Wandering with a Camera in Wales is an e
that no one should fail to take, everywher
there is unspoiled beauty and complete openness.

The whole journey has been life changing,
and a great learning experience.

For some of the shoots, I stayed in the wilds of the Brecon Beacons,
travelling through deep valleys and camping were I could find
a flat space in the rugged landscape, at times it felt almost nomadic,
but I did not wont it to end, that sense of being in the wild
and having to survive on your own was a great feeling.
Bringing back some good photographs was the icing on the cake.

The whole experience of creating images for this book
will live with me forever,
I hope you enjoy the visual experience created too.

Burial Chambers & Standing Stones

Pentre Ifan Burial Chamber

Coetan Arthur Burial Chamber St Davids Head

Gwal-y-Filiast Burial Chamber

Cereg Sampson Burial Chamber

Gwal-y-Filiast Burial Chamber

Standing Stone Cynwyl Elfed

Standing Stone Pembrokeshire Coastal Path

Pentre Ifan Burial Chamber

Pentre Ifan Burial Chamber

Cenarth Falls

Upper Ddwli Falls

Lower Ddwli Falls

Horse Shoe Falls

Swyd Gwladys Falls

Upper Clungwyn Falls

Middle Clungwyn Falls

Lower Clungwyn Falls

Brecon Beacon Fall

Brecon Beacon Fall

Brecon Beacon Falls

Victorian Dams

Craig Goch

Craig Goch

Pen-Y-Garreg Dam

Coban - Coch

Claerwen Dam

Llyn Brianne

Llyn Brianne

Animals

True Love

Ram on the Brecon Beacons

Missey My Goat

Wild Horses

Feeding Time

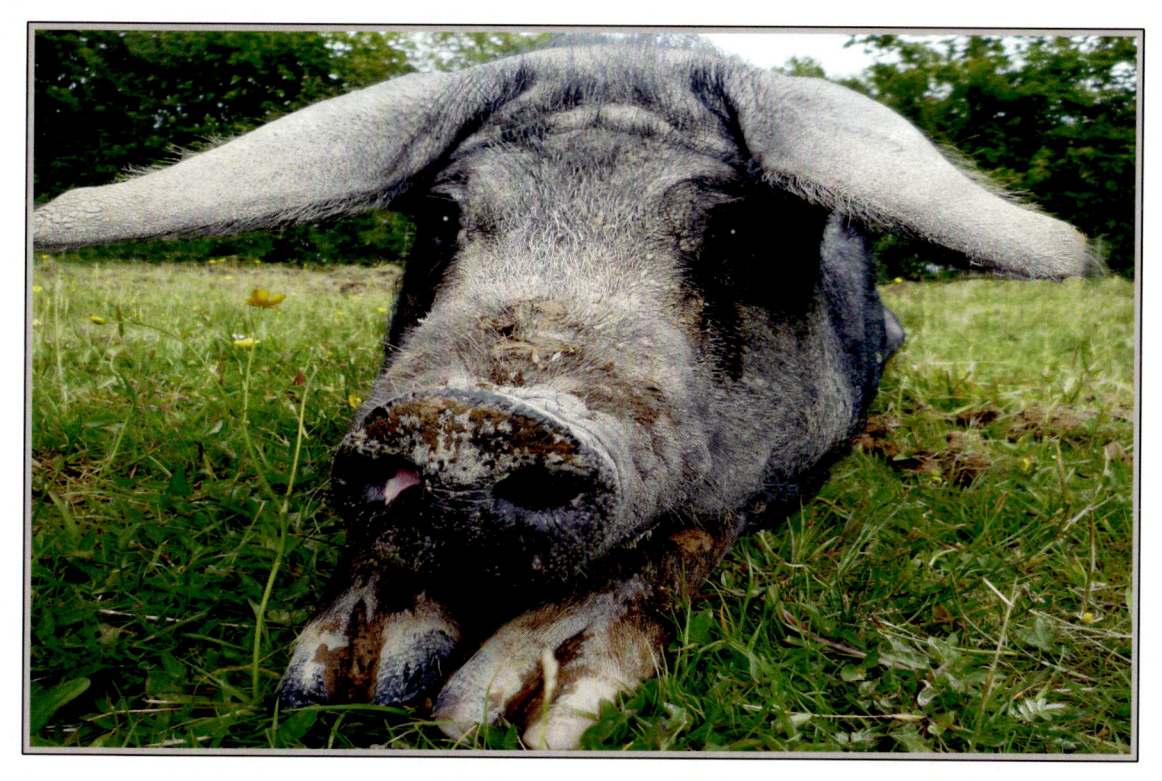

My Pet Pig

Dragon Fly

Buildings

St Davids Cathedral

In Side St Davids Cathedral

Margam

Caephilly Castle

Mwnt Church

Never to Return

Dryslwyn Castle

Landscape

Dinas Nature Reserve

A Winters Day

The Splendour of Water

The Barn Cwmduad

A Woodland Walk

Sun Set at Whitesands

Computer Art

Moon Light Night

Wondering

Not There Yet

Storm

Mistry Light

Dinefwr Manor

I would like to say thank you to all those people who have given me help during this long journey.

May I also thank all the staff at Coleg Sir Gâr, Carmarthen for their greatly needed determination in getting me through my Degree!

I hope you enjoy my journey as much as I did.